# Little Dog Rusty

# Little Dog Rusty

## Written by
### Nicole DelVecchio-Moschetti

## Illustrated by
### Jaclyn Brada

Published by Permanent Ink Press

*Little Dog Rusty*
Nicole DelVecchio Moschetti
Copyright © 2009 by Nicole DelVecchio-Moschetti
Published by Permanent Ink Press

Printed in the United States of America

*Little Dog Rusty*
Nicole DelVecchio-Moschetti

1. Title   2. Author   3. Children's Fiction

Library of Congress Control Number: 2009928084
ISBN 10: 0615296270
ISBN 13: 978-0-615-29627-2

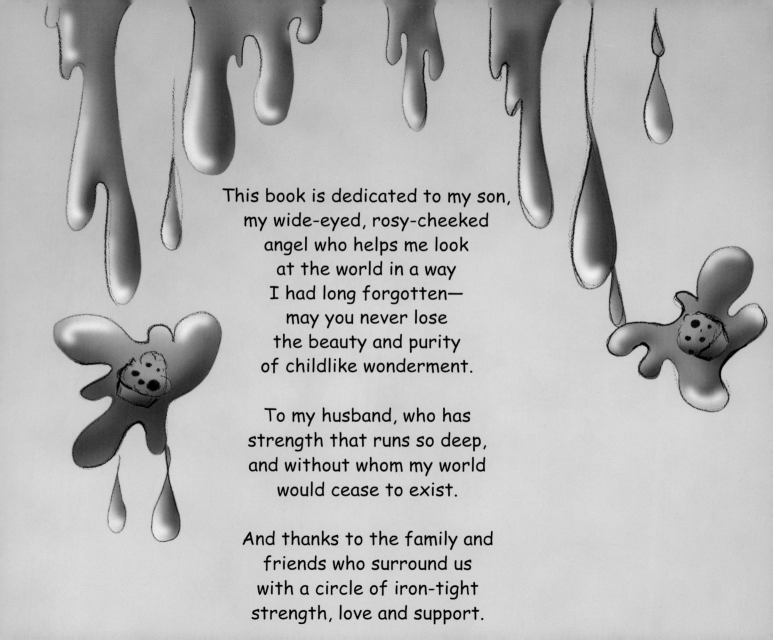

This book is dedicated to my son,
my wide-eyed, rosy-cheeked
angel who helps me look
at the world in a way
I had long forgotten—
may you never lose
the beauty and purity
of childlike wonderment.

To my husband, who has
strength that runs so deep,
and without whom my world
would cease to exist.

And thanks to the family and
friends who surround us
with a circle of iron-tight
strength, love and support.

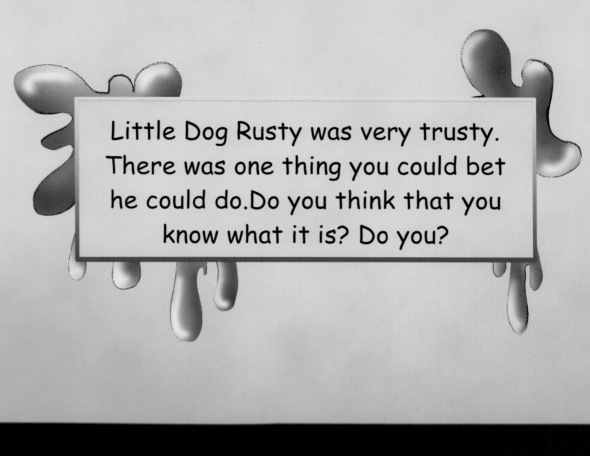

Little Dog Rusty was very trusty. There was one thing you could bet he could do.Do you think that you know what it is? Do you?

Well, you could bet that Little Dog Rusty
could always and certainly make all things messy.

His mess-making skills first were known
the very first day we brought Rusty home.

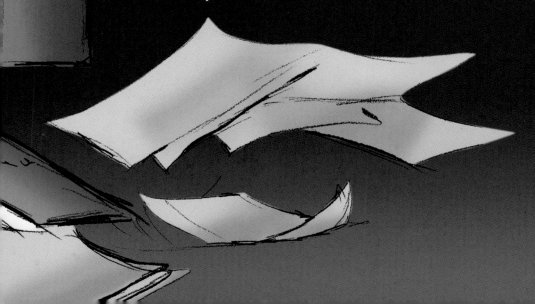

He started his mess by the coffee table.
That mess he made, we didn't think he was able.

First, he chewed up the coffee table books.
Then Nana's glasses were the next thing he took.
When she put them on they sat cockamamie.
Then Rusty moved on to my sister, Amy.

He nibbled and tugged at the socks on her feet
until he pulled them out from her, right underneath.

She hopped and she hobbled and started to wobble
and wibbled and wobbled and then she toppled.
Then poor sister Amy came crashing down
with everything else that was all around.
She pulled down the phone cord, the oven door,
the toaster, some coasters—and there's still more.
Inside that oven were blueberry muffins.
You think that sounds bad, well, honey, that's nothin'!
The mess from those muffins was almost scary,
Stained and smeared everywhere—blueberries.
And if that wasn't bad enough,
there's still a bunch of other stuff.

Inside that toaster was some bread
that landed right on Amy's head.
The next to go was the coffee pot—
still not the end, if that's what you thought.
That's when Rusty reappeared
to lick the berries that were smeared.
Then his tongue turned purple-blue,
and who do you think he gave a kiss to?
Poor sister Amy who couldn't move,
and soon her face was purple-blue.

Next Rusty had some coffee sips,
but it was hot and burnt his lips.

Little Dog Rusty
howled and moaned.
That's when Mommy
finally got home.

She looked at the mess
with complete shock—
no doubt so mad
she could hardly talk.

That's when we knew
that we were busted—
until we told her
what Rusty did.

Mommy looked
over at Rusty,
still shocked.
There he sat with
his fuzzy head
half-cocked.

He sat there so proper
on his fluffy tushie,
all sweet and innocent,
soft and smooshie.

Mommy actually started to snuggle that puppy! She couldn't believe that mess came from Rusty.

Rusty looked at her with that sweet little face while we were told to clean up the place!

Meanwhile, Amy was
stuck on her back.
That's when we started
to give her some flack.

"It's your fault, you
pulled all this down
when you fell!"
"Rusty tripped me, it's
his fault!" she yelled.

We started by snuggling
and brushing his fluff.
Belly-up on the floor,
he wasn't so tough.

We threw and he fetched
his little toy rope.
Was he messing the house
up right now? Nope.

When given a little
doggie treat, he sat.
Still making no messes,
how about that?

Thinking our job of taming Rusty was done, we went outside to ride bikes for some fun.

Twenty minutes later we came back in and couldn't believe where Rusty had been.

We saw that Rusty had jumped onto the chair. Do you know where he went once he got there?

From there he jumped onto the counter!
I thought of Mommy and went and found her.

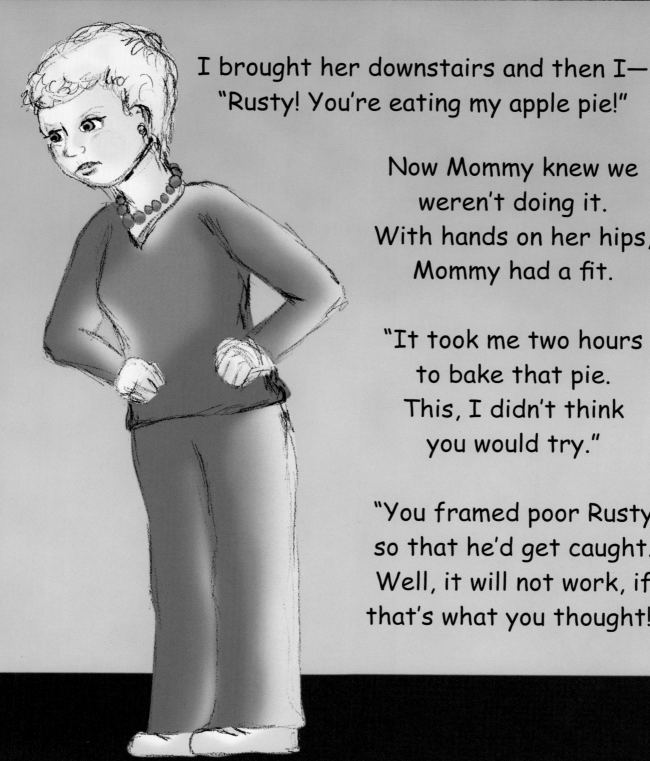

I brought her downstairs and then I—
"Rusty! You're eating my apple pie!"

Now Mommy knew we
weren't doing it.
With hands on her hips,
Mommy had a fit.

"It took me two hours
to bake that pie.
This, I didn't think
you would try."

"You framed poor Rusty
so that he'd get caught.
Well, it will not work, if
that's what you thought!"

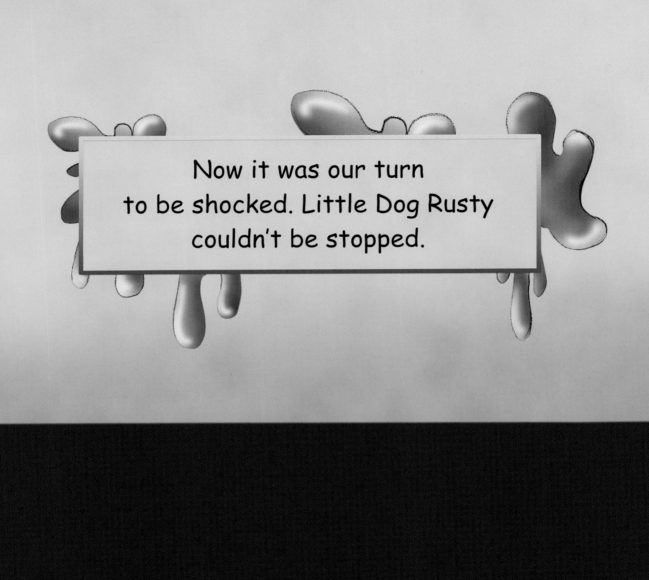

Now it was our turn
to be shocked. Little Dog Rusty
couldn't be stopped.

The End